The Prayer Track!

GOD, I REALLY NEED TO TALK TO YOU!

HOW TO PRAY

By Bernard Smalls

6 Laps to Daily Spiritual Fitness

ISBN Number: 978-0-557-26137-6

Printed in the United States of America
Published by: O. Bernard Smalls

The Prayer Track!

-- ACKNOWLEDGEMENT --

I want to acknowledge Dr. David Y. Cho of Seoul, Korea as my pastor and prayer mentor. Much of what I share in these lessons I learned directly from this humble man who changed the nation of Korea through prayer. We have nothing to share that we did not learn, so always I like to give credit to my teachers or mentors whom I lean heavily upon in various areas of my life. I believe that we are to share what we learn from our mentors. Why reinvent the wheel? Paul said we are to commit what we have learned to faithful men who will teach others also.

And the things that you have heard from me among many witnesses, commit these to faithful men who will be able to teach others also. 2 Timothy 2:2 (New King James Version)

Preface

Understanding how to pray has been the greatest spiritual challenge facing humanity. Many have gone from one extreme to another seeking solutions to the prayer problem. I have personally had my own journey of adventure and I must admit discouragement in seeking how to pray. After much study, frustration, despair, and hundreds of prayer meetings, and many years of searching, I have come to my own conclusion on the simple solution to a productive prayer life. Finding the answer was greatly influenced by the teachings of my pastor and spiritual mentor, Dr. David Yonggi Cho. I heard Dr. Cho teach a simple lesson entitled "How to Pray" and it changed my entire prayer life. I thought, since he is the pastor of the world's largest single church congregation, I should listen to what he had to say about prayer. In this message he taught us how he prays daily and gave many practical illustrations and answers to building a prayer life. The answers, he said, are in what we have traditionally call the Lord's prayer. The solution is found in the principles from the teaching of Jesus on how to pray. I have written this book for one simple reason, and that is, to motivate and teach people *how to pray*.

In this manner, therefore, pray:

Our Father in heaven, Hallowed be Your name.

Your kingdom come. Your will be done, on earth as it is in heaven. Give us this day our daily bread.

And forgive us our debts, As we forgive our debtors.

And do not lead us into temptation, But deliver us from the evil one. For Yours is the kingdom and the power and the glory forever. Amen.

Matthew 6:9-13 (New King James Version)

MOTIVATING PEOPLE TO PRAY

GOD, I REALLY NEED TO TALK TO YOU!

If My people who are called by My name will humble themselves, and pray and seek My face, and turn from their wicked ways, then I will hear from heaven, and will forgive their sin and heal their land. 2 Chronicles 7:14 (New King James Version)

If we really understood the massive benefits of prayer, I believe we would all do it more. James 5:13 says, "Is any one of you in trouble? *He should pray.* Is anyone happy? Let him sing songs of praise." One major prayer motivator is trouble. Even those who never pray during ordinary times will pray earnestly during suffering, because they urgently need help. When we are in trouble, we all say either consciously or subconsciously, "God, I really need to talk to You!" As the old saying goes, "there are no atheists in a foxhole." Psalm 50:15 says, "...and call upon me in the day of trouble; I will deliver you, and you will honor me." When we call upon God in trouble or tribulation, God will deliver us. John Bunyan said, *"Trials and tribulation make us seek God."*

THE VALUE OF TRIALS

In normal times, people do not tend to seek God, but they cling to God during trials. Babies do not need their mother if they are full. Hunger makes them cry for their mother. When your children who are far away suddenly write, email, or call you, saying, "I love you Mom and Dad. I respect you," then you should know that they need money! If everything is okay, your children may not think of you. You may not hear from them even once a year. However, in the midst of suffering, they become busy, giving you several calls, and sending you frequent emails.

We also seek God and cry out to Him in the midst of suffering. Martin Luther said, *"The most peaceful time without trials is the most serious crisis, for people are tempted to forget about God."* Trials are valuable because they often cause us to seek God. Being human, it is easy to kick back and relax when all is going well. James spoke of the value of test and trials in James chapter 1.

James, a servant of God and of the Lord Jesus Christ, To the twelve tribes scattered among the nations: Greetings. 2 Consider it pure joy, my brothers, whenever you face trials of many kinds, 3 because you know that the testing of your faith develops perseverance. James 1:1-3 (New International Version)

CRISIS LEADS TO PRAYER

Your easy life can be one of the greatest hindrances to your prayer life. If there is no trial but only peace, people tend to forget God and not pray. This is the problem with the American Church. Therefore, spiritually speaking a period without trials can be more threatening than a period with suffering. If there are trials and suffering, people become broken, obedient, careful, and cry out to God. Otherwise, they tend to be arrogant, haughty, and self-indulgent. C.S. Lewis said, *"Why does suffering exist? Most people are indifferent to the voice of God until some crisis comes to them. Suffering is God's loudspeaker through which He delivers His will to them."*

God shouts through His loudspeaker, "Listen to me!" Through suffering, God shouts with a loud voice to make us repent and follow His will. Before suffering, we tend to turn a deaf ear to God. Without suffering, we will not obey God. Don't think for a moment, "Bernard prays because he is so religious or spiritual." To be totally transparent, I often pray mostly because I need God's help facing this crisis called life. I say, God! I really need talk to you when I face a crisis. Crisis in the Chinese language means *dangerous wind* or *danger yet opportunity*. Crisis is God's opportunity to show you great and mighty things as you pray.

UNDERSTANDING SUFFERING

Dr. Cho says, "Suffering is our prayer instructor." In normal times when people are asked to pray, they say, "I am too pressed for time. I am so tired and busy now!" It is amazing how we are too busy to pray until some extreme trouble strikes. The Bible offers us prayer as God's way to get out of trouble. Many will try anything when trouble hits if they believe it will work.

Trouble can be a great motivator to pray. Prayer is one way that you can make lemonade when life throws you lemons. The good thing about trouble is that it can be a motivator to pray.

Prayer motivation often works best in times of trouble. Why? We are always motivated to move away from pain and toward pleasure in life. It is called the pain-pleasure principle. Motivation is a powerful concept. Let me illustrate with a story that I shared in my book, *The Lemonade Principle*:

> A Texan who has an intelligent, beautiful daughter wanted her to marry a winner, so he invited the most eligible bachelors in the state to a party.
>
> He said to them, "If you can swim across my Olympic-sized swimming pool (filled with alligators and crocodiles), you will have a choice of selecting either one million dollars, 10,000 acres of land, or my daughter's hand in marriage." Immediately there was a splash in the water, then a gentleman came up on the opposite side of the pool.

The Texan asked him, "Do you want a million dollars?"

"No," he replied.

"Do you want 10,000 acres of land?"

"No!" he said again.

With a smile on his face, the Texan said, "Then you want my daughter's hand in marriage?"

"NO!" the man shouted.

Frustrated, the Texan asked, "Then what do you want?" With an angry snarl on his face the man replied, *"I want to know who pushed me in!"* That's called fear motivation. It works. Many times we are motivated to pray when we find ourselves swimming in alligators and crocodiles, which represents a life of tests and trials.

AFTER YOU HAVE SUFFERED A WHILE...

1 Peter 5:10 says, "And the God of all grace, who called you to his eternal glory in Christ, after you have suffered a little while, will himself restore you and make you strong, firm and steadfast." Suffering makes us strong, firm, and steadfast. Do not boast about having no suffering in your life. It is far more dangerous without suffering than with it. Here is a saying I learned years ago in the world of corporate training: *"Nothing fails like success!"* Even in business, suffering and trouble makes us sharper and stronger. Crisis and suffering can make us better when it inspires us to pray. For the Christian, trouble is the wake-up call to pray. Are you suffering in your finances, health, or relationships? The seed of the greater benefit for you is **prayer motivation**. Psalm 119:71 says, "It was good for me to be afflicted so that I might learn your decrees."

"Every adversity carries within it the seed of equal or greater benefit."
-- Napoleon Hill

WHY SHOULD WE PRAY?

And call upon me in the day of trouble. Psalm 50:15

The understanding of why we should pray is very important if we are going to maintain a consistent prayer life. I am taking some time motivating you to pray. I have learned through my practical experience as a pastor that people will pray if provided proper motivation to pray. In my Church in Alaska, we had early prayer at 5:00 a.m. six days a week and all night prayer once a month on a Friday night. Every meeting was attended by numerous Christians who enjoyed these prayer times because they were *motivated* to pray and experienced many miracles and answers to prayer. When we know why you should do something and see the benefit in doing it, this naturally creates motivation to do it. Psychology teaches that when we have a sound mind, it is impossible to be highly motivated to do something that will only cause us harm. We are always motivated to move toward what causes pleasure.

THE PLEASURE PRINCIPLE

The **pleasure principle** is a psychoanalytic concept, originated by famous psychologist Sigmund Freud._The **pleasure principle** states that people seek pleasure and avoid pain, i.e. people seek to satisfy biological and psychological needs. The counterpart is the reality principle, which defers gratification when necessary. An individual follows the pleasure principle in early life, but as one matures one learns the need to endure pain and defer gratification, because of the exigencies and obstacles of reality. In Freud's words, an ego thus educated has become *reasonable*; it no longer lets itself be governed by the pleasure principle., Instead it obeys the reality principle, which also at bottom seeks to obtain pleasure. This is how prayer works as we grow and mature in the Lord. As spiritual babies and children, all we want is pleasure, material blessings and things that are good to the flesh. As we grow in the Lord, we learn that to have true and proper pleasure, prosperity, and success, we must sometimes defer gratification and endure pain while seeking God in prayer.

Very few Christians today are willing to bear pain. As we say in the world of fitness: no pain, no gain. Moses understood this principle. It contributed to his closeness to God. He chose to deny immediate pleasure for long-term pleasure.

By faith Moses, when he was come to years, refused to be called the son of Pharaoh's daughter; Choosing rather to suffer affliction with the people of God, than to enjoy the pleasures of sin for a season; Esteeming the reproach of Christ greater riches than the treasures in Egypt: for he had respect unto the recompence of the reward. By faith he forsook Egypt, not fearing the wrath of the king: for he endured, as seeing him who is invisible. Hebrews 11:24-27 (King James Version)

PRAYER DELIVERS US FROM TROUBLE

Another reason why we should pray is that prayer delivers us from trouble. The Bible instructs us to call upon God in the day of trouble. Job 5:7 says that man is born to trouble just as surely as sparks fly upward. When there is a fire, the flames shoot upward. Among us today, regardless of who we are, I am sure we have suffered, perhaps to different degrees. While God has sent the sinless man Jesus Christ to this world, He has never created anyone who did not suffer some hardship. When we face hardship, we must not think we are the only ones who are suffering. We must not despair or lose hope. When facing hardship we must examine our hearts, use the opportunity to repent, pray, and abandon our disobedience and lack of faith. Trouble is often a time for us to think deeply about our God.

THE LORD WILL PROVIDE (Jehovah-Jireh)

God is Jehovah-Jireh. When we face hardship we must remember that God will provide a way for us. Knowing this we can find strength and courage through prayer. Abraham took the son he begot at age 100 to Mt. Moriah to build an altar and sacrifice his son Isaac upon that altar; it was God's command. Abraham must have felt deep despair and indescribable loss. But he had to obey God's command, which would mean the death of his son. How could he obey this command? Being faced with this, he may even have wanted to die himself. However, he took his son on a three-day journey to Mt. Moriah, and they built an altar together. He placed Isaac on that altar, and just as he was ready to plunge the knife into his son's heart, God provided a way out of this predicament. It is written in Genesis 22:12-14, "'Do not lay a hand on the boy,' he said. 'Do not do anything to him. Now I know that you fear God, because you have not withheld from me your son, your only son.' Abraham looked up and there in a thicket he saw a ram caught by its horns. He went over and took the ram and sacrificed it as a burnt offering instead of his son. So Abraham called that place **The LORD Will Provide**. And to this day it is said, 'On the mountain of the LORD it will be provided.'"

GOD PROVIDES A WAY OUT AS WE PRAY

As Abraham faced the great turmoil of having to sacrifice his son, God provided a way out. God provided an animal to be sacrificed in Isaac's place so that his life could be spared. When we face hardship and tribulation with prayer, God does indeed provide a way out. Just as God prepared a ram to be sacrificed in Isaac's place, He provides a way out for us. It is written in 1 Corinthians 10:13, "No temptation has seized you except what is common to man. And God is faithful; he will not let you be tempted beyond what you can bear. But when you are tempted, he will also provide a way out so that you can stand up under it if we pray. Because God knows our weaknesses, He does not allow us to be faced with hardship that we cannot overcome. Prayer is often the way of escape.

HARDSHIP MOTIVATES US TO PRAY

Dr. Cho tells the story of when he was a student in elementary school and lived in the country. He said; "On the way to school, I used to pass a field. In the spring it was filled with sprouts. Dragonflies used to climb on those sprouts. One morning on the way to school, I saw a dragonfly emerging; it was struggling because its caterpillar skin was hard to shed. Its head was out but it was struggling. So I thought I would show it mercy and I tore the skin and gave it its freedom. I went happily on my way. On my way back home, I came to the same spot and saw a large gathering of ants; they were all over the dragonfly, tearing it to pieces. That dragonfly couldn't fly. Although I didn't know it at the time, I learned later that when a dragonfly struggles, a slick of oil is produced which is applied over the wings and body. Once the oil dries, the dragonfly can open its wings and fly into the sky. If the dragonfly does not struggle, the oil is not produced and the wings wither under the sunlight; it becomes food for the ants. I wasn't being merciful; I had brought death to the dragonfly."

Hardship is much like the dragonfly that sheds its caterpillar skin. Through hardship, we are able to repent and surrender ourselves to obedience so that we may open our wings of faith and prayer. As such, Christians become transformed and mature through hardship. That is why God allows us to pass through the tunnels of hardship and suffering. We must always realize, however, that God has already prepared a way for us through that suffering and hardship. Prayer helps us to find the way to victory. God is the source of our courage and strength. Although the world may be filled with darkness and no escape in sight, we must realize that God has already prepared a way out for us.

Although our eyes may not see it or our ears hear it or our senses feel it, we must remember our God who provides a way out for us as we pray. **This is why we should pray.** We should call upon the Lord in the day of trouble and He will deliver us. What trouble are you facing that you need to pray about today? I encourage you to call upon Him today, and make prayer a habit in your life.

START YOUR DAY RIGHT

I encourage you to start off each day by praying this simple prayer, even if you just read it out loud and watch the miracles start to emerge in your life. I will share why this prayer is so effective later in the book. But for now, here it is:

9 In this manner, therefore, pray: Our Father in heaven, Hallowed be Your name. 10
Your kingdom come. Your will be done, On earth as it is in heaven. 11 Give us this day
our daily bread. 12 And forgive us our debts, As we forgive our debtors. 13 And do not
lead us into temptation, But deliver us from the evil one. For Yours is the kingdom and
the power and the glory forever. Amen. Matthew 6:9-13 (New King James Version)

Answering The Call to Pray

Lord, teach us to pray... Luke 11:1

Jesus is the undisputed greatest teacher in the history of the world. I think most people would agree with that. However, not many know *why* He was such a great teacher. Let me explain. He was a Master Teacher of course because He was anointed by the Holy Spirit to teach, but in a practical sense He also understood how people learn. People learn when a teacher starts with what they are familiar with to take them into what they are not familiar with.

Great teachers start with what is known and try to teach us the unknown. The net result is that we learn something new. Jesus taught continually in parables. A parable is simply a story that reveals a spiritual truth that is parallel with a truth in the natural world. Since the learner understands the natural truth, the parable makes it easy to understand the spiritual. The reason parables are so effective is that they bridge the knowledge *gap* between the known and the unknown, the spiritual and the natural. In essence, teaching is taking a student from the known to the unknown.

Jesus taught the people of his day by simply starting with what they knew, such as farming, planting seeds, different types of soil, fishing and so forth, to teach spirituality. So, if you understood farming, He made easy for you to understand spiritual growth and prayer. Many today try to teach deep spiritual truths by starting with what people *don't know*. This is the root cause for much confusion in the Church. We must start with the known to take people into deeper spirituality.

SIMPLICITY = POWER

I have caused my share of confusion because I was trying to sound deep. I later discovered that the power is in simplicity because it starts with the obvious, the known to bridge the gap to the unknown.

For example, when Jesus said the Kingdom of heaven is like a big net, He was speaking their language because His audiences were very familiar with *fishing*. Fishing was one of the top trades of the times. Remember, Peter, James, and John, three of his first disciples, were fishermen. Jesus always used a *simple* natural parallel. So to understand prayer we need a parallel, a natural illustration or truth to be the bridge to the spiritual. Matthew 4:18-22 (NIV) says, "As Jesus was walking beside the Sea of Galilee, he saw two brothers, Simon called Peter and his brother Andrew. They were casting a net into the lake, for they were fishermen. 'Come, follow me,' Jesus said, 'and I will make you fishers of men.' At once they left their nets and followed him. Going on from there, he saw two other brothers, James son of Zebedee and his brother John. They were in a boat with their father Zebedee, preparing their nets. Jesus called them, and immediately they left the boat and their father and followed him."

Jesus knew that his disciples understood fishing, so He taught many lessons that started with the concept of fishing to teach deeper truths. He even taught salvation by saying, "follow me and I will make you *fishers* of men."

THE TRACK ANALOGY

The analogy or parallel I want to use in this book is that of a *track,* as used in track and field, or sports. Close your eyes and imagine a track that is designed for running laps. Maybe your mind goes back to high school or even college. See the track in your mind's eye. Now, use your imagination to see yourself preparing to run the six (6) laps. You would of course make sure that you were properly hydrated. You would drink some water before running. You would then relax and prepare mentally for enduring. You might even see yourself crossing the finish line in advance.

What Jesus taught in the Lord's Prayer lays out a spiritual track for us to run. It is like a Prayer Track that has six laps. I call these six (6) *laps* to daily spiritual fitness. Start to look at prayer as your spiritual fitness program, not as something you must do to get God to love you. God loves you unconditionally no matter how much or how little you pray. This is about your spiritual fitness, not earning God's love.

Just as you would plan your jog in the natural world, plan your prayer! Jesus gave us six (6) laps to run to stay spiritually fit. Notice that I am using the term jog. Prayer is more like a jog than a sprint. Slow down, prepare, take you time and enjoy the jog!

THE 6 LAPS TO DAILY SPIRITUAL FITNESS

1) Our Father in heaven, Hallowed be Your name.

2) Your kingdom come. Your will be done, On earth as it is in heaven.

3) Give us this day our daily bread.

4) And forgive us our debts, As we forgive our debtors.

5) And do not lead us into temptation, But deliver us from the evil one.

6) For Yours is the kingdom and the power and the glory forever. Amen.

WHAT IS PRAYER?

'Call to Me, and I will answer you, and show you great and mighty things, which you do not know.' Jeremiah 33:3 (New King James Version)

Prayer is a business meeting with God. You could say prayer is simply *communicating* with God. A civilization is only as great as its communication system. In modern warfare, one of the first rules of engagement is to knock out or destroy the communication system of the enemy. When communication is destroyed, the opposing army is always at a severe disadvantage.

God wants you to talk to or communicate with Him *regularly*. This will give you a definite advantage of victory over your enemy, Satan. We call this type of communication prayer. Prayer is communicating with God. **God has invited you to communicate with Him.**

He wants you to call unto Him in prayer so that He can show you great things that you do not know. He wants you to know how to pray so that He can show you great things.

THE PRAYER MODEL

Jesus kept prayer simple. Why? In simplicity lays the power. He gave us what I call the *prayer model* in Matthew chapter 6. It is a model that is so simple I memorized it as a child. The thing that really got my attention about this prayer was listening to Dr. Yonggi Cho, the pastor of the world's largest church, teach about how he prays. Dr. Cho is the pastor of a church with over 700,000 members in Seoul, Korea, which is a *world-renowned* church of prayer.

I heard him teach in Seattle, Washington, in the late 1980s. Later I heard a cassette tape entitled "How to Pray" by this great pastor. I must admit that at first I was disappointed when Dr. Cho, after announcing his topic as How To Pray, went right into teaching what we know as the Lord's Prayer. I wanted something spiritual, something *deep,* and not some teaching on the Lord's Prayer.
Dr. Cho went on to say that if he prays three times in a day, he prays this same prayer pattern, as he called it. He just runs the same *laps*, over and over.

As I listened, I had an a-ha moment. The power was in simplicity. I thoughtfully considered that if anyone alive knows how to pray it must be Dr. Cho, the pastor of the world's largest church. At the time, his church in Korea was winning over 10,000 new souls per month.

Then, I thought about the fact that South Korea was considered the greatest economic miracle in the history of the world, which Dr. Cho has attributed to the spiritual revival, the result of which is prayer. I believe the United States now needs this type of revival.

So I decided to personally start praying this prayer. I started praying it almost verbatim and began to see results the first day. Now I personally pray this prayer every morning before starting my day. I experience God's miracles daily, even when I least expect them, and I know it is a result of praying this prayer, which is based on His priorities.

PRAYER AND THE GRACE OF GOD

Beloved, I pray that you may prosper in all things and be in health, just as your soul prospers. 3 John 1:2 (New King James Version)

There are five facets of God's grace manifested in our redemption in Christ. Redemption means to buy back. God has bought us back from the enemy by the precious blood of Jesus. In Biblical numerology, five is the number of grace. God has declared a threefold blessing because of His grace according to 3 John 2. Three is the number of God.

The threefold blessings are *prosperity*, *health,* and *salvation,* or prosperity of the soul. Ephesians 2:8 says, "for **it is by grace you have been saved, through faith and this not from yourselves, it is the gift of God."** One classical definition of grace, which I learned in bible college, is that grace is God's unmerited favor. A more exacting definition of grace that I learned as I grew spiritually is, "Grace is God's willingness to use His power in our behalf, even though we don't deserve it." Let me illustrate it this way: I may be in *favor* of you having one thousand dollars, but on the other hand, I may not be *willing* to use my power to give you the money.

Grace is God's *willingness* to use His power on your behalf, even though you don't deserve it! Remember that five is the number of grace, and the redemptive Names of God reveal to us the five-faceted grace of redemption. or you could say the love of God to man. God is good! He loves you just as you are and wants you to experience His grace in five basic areas today.

FIVE = GRACE

We are using an S word for each benefit to aid your memory. The Bible says forget not all of His benefits. Let us not forget any of His five-faceted benefits. I am grateful to Dr. Larry Lea for his teaching in his excellent book, *Could You Not Tarry One Hour?*, for the five S insight.

The five S words help us to remember the benefits of redemption. **He Gives More Grace.** Where sin abounds, grace abounds much more. We should continue confessing the five benefits God's grace in prayer. Hebrews 13:15 says, "Through Jesus, therefore, let us continually offer to God a sacrifice of praise, the fruit of lips that confess his name." Notice in Hebrews 13:15 the words: praise, fruit of our lips, and confess. Confession is a form of prayer and praise. God loves you and He wants you to experience His grace in five basic areas; these things belong to you by faith. It is up to you to declare and claim the benefits in prayer.

Let us not forget any of His five-faceted benefits. The five S words help us remember the benefits of redemption.

The first S is for Sin

Thank God that you are free from sin and sin consciousness.

The second S is Spirit

Acknowledge His benefit and thank God for this facet of redemption. Let today be a day of peace in His presence.

The third S is for Security

Divine security is freedom from fear of man, terrorism or loss.

The fourth S is for Soundness

Praise His Name for health, healing, and soundness, for redeeming you from Sickness and disease and giving me Divine health. Divine health is freedom from disease.

The fifth S is for Success

Your confession of faith works an eternal value in you and produces prosperity. Praise Him for it. Today is a day of Divine prosperity and freedom from poverty and lack.
Forget not all of His benefits!

Running The Prayer Track

Lap #1 Our Father in heaven, Hallowed be Your name

Who has ascended into heaven, or descended? Who has gathered the wind in His fists? Who has bound the waters in a garment? Who has established all the ends of the earth? What *is* His name, and what *is* His Son? Name, If you know? Proverbs 30:4 (New King James Version)

I have always found the preceding verse intriguing. *What is His Name and what is His Son's Name?* This is poetic revelation. It puts emphasis on the importance of knowing **His Name and His Son's Name**. We are to start on our prayer track by praising and worshiping His Name. What is the place of significance of His Name and His Son's Name? Philippians 2:9-11 says, "Wherefore also God highly exalted him, and gave unto him the name which is above every name that in the name of Jesus every knee should bow, of things in heaven and things on earth and things under the earth, and that every tongue should confess that Jesus Christ is Lord, to the glory of God the Father." He has the Name above every name in the three worlds: Heaven, Earth, and Hell. He has inherited by conquest God's Name! Every demon and angel is subject to the Imperial Name of Jesus and, wonder of wonders, He gave us the Power of Attorney to use that Name of Might.

HIS NAME

All of our Authority is based on His finished work, but it is all enwrapped in His name. By His giving to us the legal use of this name, He has put omnipotence at our disposal in our combat with Satanic hosts. Mark 16:17-20: "And these signs shall accompany them that believe: in my name shall they cast out demons; they shall speak with new tongues; they shall take up serpents, and if they drink any deadly thing, it shall in no wise hurt them; they shall lay hands on the sick, and they shall recover. So then the Lord Jesus, after he had spoken unto them, was received up into heaven and sat down at the right hand of God. And they went forth, and preached everywhere, the Lord working with them, and confirming the word by the signs that followed. In my name shall they cast out demons." Here He defines our *Legal Authority*. We shall cast out demons (this means Authority over demons in their relation to men), cast them out of peoples' bodies; break their power over those bodies, minds, and spirits; break their power over meetings, homes, and sometimes communities.

Our combat is not against flesh and blood but against the principalities, and powers in heavenly places; in other words, our war is against demons of all ranks, kinds, and authorities. They are attacking the human everywhere, especially the children of God. How are we to defend ourselves against them, or lead an assault on their hosts, and deliver the captives? The air is pregnant with evil spirits who seek to infest our bodies as bats do old buildings.

IN MY NAME

The awful power of evil in our land eloquently proves what we write. "In my Name ye shall speak in new tongues." This new and startling manifestation of the Spirit is our Legal Right in the Name, where all the mighty powers of God are kept for us. "In my Name they shall take up serpents, and if they drink any deadly thing it shall not harm them. They shall lay hands on the sick, and they shall recover." Here it is not sufferance or pity, but Legal Authority. You have as much right to demand healing as you have to demand the cashing of a check at a bank where you have an account. You have a Legal Right to deliverance from Satan. This legal right is called *redemption*. The grace of God through His Name is revealed in the plan of redemption. Prayer is the key to manifesting your redemption and enjoying the five benefits of redemption.

CONFESSING HIS NAME IN PRAYER

Through Jesus, therefore, let us continually offer to God a sacrifice of praise—the fruit of lips that confess his name. Hebrews 13:15 (New International Version)

What is God's Name? God has a multifaceted Name. His Name is manifested in varied names to describe the benefits of His goodness and redemptive nature. I am indebted to the work of Dr. David Y. Cho and Dr. Larry Lea for their insight on these five benefits, which they both tied to the compound redemptive Names of Jehovah God. As mentioned earlier, in his classic book, *Could You Not Tarry One Hour?*, Dr. Lea identifies the five benefits as SIN, SPIRIT, SECURITY, SOUNDNESS, and SUCCESS. Dr. Lea admits that he learned this revelation from Dr. Cho. Dr. Cho calls these five benefits the five facets of the full gospel.

They are the five basic benefits of redemption to all humanity. In classical theology, each name begins with the Hebrew name Jehovah, meaning THE LORD, which is then compounded with the part of the Name that describes the benefit. They are known as compound names. For example, Jehovah-jireh is the compound name for, "The Lord our provider". The five-faceted grace of God produces a threefold blessing as described in 3 John 2: "Beloved, I pray that you may prosper in all things and be in health, just as your soul prospers."

GOD'S NAME(s) REVEALS HIS LOVE FOR YOU!

Beloved, I pray that you may prosper in all things and be in health, just as your soul prospers. 3 John 1:2 (New King James Version)

The 3-fold Blessings That Belongs to You Are :

1. Prosperity—a material blessing

2. Health—a physical blessing

3. Salvation—a spiritual blessing

In 1 John 4:8, the Bible says that God is love! Since God is love, everything about Him reflects love, even His Name. God has provided for us redemption because of His love. Redemption basically means to buy back. It is best illustrated by a how a pawnshop works. When you put your property or goods into a pawnshop, you have to pay the price to redeem them or buy them back. God has bought us back from the enemy by the precious blood of Jesus. There are five facets of God's grace manifested in our redemption in Christ. God has declared a threefold blessing because of His grace according to 3 John 2. The blessings are prosperity, health, and salvation or prosperity of the soul. His Name(s) mean BLESSINGS TO YOU!

THIS BLOOD'S FOR YOU!

Then they are to take some of the blood and put it on the sides and tops of the doorframes of the houses where they eat the lambs. Exodus 12:7 (New International Version)

The blood is the path of approach into God's presence in prayer. Christ's blood is definitive proof of God's love for all humanity, no matter who you are or what you have done! Just as the high priest of old could not enter God's presence without blood (of animals used for religious sacrifice), neither can we enter His presence today in prayer without faith in the blood of Jesus, the Sacrifice Lamb of God, that washed away our sins. The blood cleanses your conscience and gives you confidence and boldness to approach God. Imagine that the blood that has cleansed you, and is cleansing you from ALL of your sin as you start out in prayer!

Now confess, "This blood is for me! His blood is now cleansing me from all sin consciousness!" Relax, imagine, and enjoy His cleansing. This will give you confidence and boldness before the Throne of grace. Faith in His blood gives us access to God as we pray. Imagine His Blood. Thank God for the blood! Confess the blood!

THE BLOOD IS THE WAY!

The religious leaders of the day accused the early disciples of attempting to bring this man's blood upon them. That's right! It is the Father's desire to bring this Man's blood upon all humanity because it cleanses man from sin. This Blood is for you! Now confess, “His Blood is for me.” In prayer you should praise and hallow the Names of God through and by the blood of Jesus! Simply say through the blood of Jesus, “I praise and worship your Name!”

Remember to keep the word of faith in your mouth today and to write down your revelations and insights in your personal journal. Habakkuk 2:2 says, "Write the vision."

Confess your redemption today as you pray. Say: *I am an overcomer by the blood of the Lamb and the confession of God's Word. I am a winner today by the blood.*

THE CHART OF HIS NAME(s)

Here is a chart of the compound names of Jehovah and the corresponding meaning which implies a benefit. There are eight compound names. Eight is the number of completion or new beginnings. I will simply introduce the Names today, and in a later teaching I will show you how to appropriate each Name. Start meditating today upon the Name, the benefit and the redemptive fact and praise His Name! The Names work in sync with the Threefold Blessing: 1) Prosperity 2) Divine Health 3) Salvation

The Name, the Benefit, & the Redemptive Facet

1 Jehovah-Tsidkenu:	Our Righteousness
2 Jehovah-M'Kaddesh:	Our Sanctification
3 Jehovah-Shalom:	Our Peace
4 Jehovah-Shammah:	Our Ever Present One
5 Jehovah-Rohi:	Our Shepherd
6 Jehovah-Nissi:	Our Victory/Banner
7 Jehovah-Rophe:	Our Healer
8 Jehovah-Jireh:	Our Provider

Confess this now: By the blood of Jesus the Name(s) of God meets every need in my life. I confess and live the in power of God's Name! His Name is my protection and my success.

Visualize Your Blessings! Close your eyes and visualize yourself as redeemed from all harm, loss, sickness, poverty, and failure! This is God's will for you, even if you are going through a tough time now. God loves you, even His Name reflect His personal love for you!

THE NAMES & THE BENEFITS

Jehovah-Tsidkenu: Our Righteousness

'This is the name they'll give him: 'God-Who-Puts-Everything-Right.' Jeremiah 23:6 (The Message)

CONFESSING GOD'S FIVE FACET GRACE IN PRAYER

Ephesians 2:8 (NIV) says, "For it is by grace you have been saved, through faith-and this not from yourselves, it is the gift of God." Grace is God's willingness to use His power in our behalf, even though we don't deserve it. Five is the number of grace in Biblical numerology, and the Names of God reveal to us the five-faceted grace of redemption, or you could say, the love of God to man. Now that we have an overview of the Names, let's focus on confessing the five benefits. God is good! He loves you just as you are and wants you to experience His grace in five basic areas today. Remember, we are using an "S" word for each benefit to aid your memory. The Bible says forget not all of His benefits. Let us not forget any of His five-faceted benefits, or the five "S" words to help us remember the benefits of redemption.

The first "S" is for **Sin**.

The first redemptive name of God is *Jehovah-Tsidkenu* (pronounced sid-k-new); meaning the Lord Our Righteousness. No one of us is righteous in ourselves. We are all sinners saved by grace. None are good enough without God's favor and love. So He is our righteousness! **Jeremiah 23:6 (The Message) says, "This is the name they'll give him: 'God-Who-Puts-Everything-Right.'"**

Simply say, "You are Jehovah-Tsidkenu, The Lord my Righteousness." Jehovah-Tsidkenu, I confess Your Name by the blood of Jesus! Now thank and praise God that you are free from sin and sin consciousness. Say, "**You are the God Who puts everything right in my life!"**

Since you are running prayer laps, if you let me, I will coach you in prayer to help you get started! In track and field we have track coaches, don't we? Coaches make life easier because they have experience in the area under study. First, you should simply remember and visualize the blood of Jesus and declare or proclaim the Name! Your words have power. Proverbs 18:20 says, "Death and life are in the power of the tongue." Again, let me illustrate. Say out loud, "You are Jehovah-Tsidkenu, The Lord my Righteousness. I praise Your Name for redeeming me from sin." Then by faith, imagine yourself as totally righteous, because you are! Remember to imagine the blood of Jesus. While you relax, just dwell on the Name; The Lord our Righteousness, and see yourself as the righteousness of God in Christ (2 Corintheans 5:21). We were all sinners until we came to the blood. Never forget it is the Blood of Jesus that made you righteous. It is the grace of God. Praise His Name! God dwells in the praises of His people. Today I want you to enjoy God's Presence and His righteousness!

Lap #1 Our Father in heaven, Hallowed be Your Name

SEPARATED FROM THE EVILS OF A NEGATIVE WORLD

And you shall keep My statutes and do them. I am the Lord Who sanctifies you.
Leviticus 20:8 (Amplified Bible)

Many believers have a sense of unworthiness and sin-consciousness. Christ's blood has put us all on a level playing field and made us all worthy. Why? He is the Lamb of God who takes away **the sin of the whole world**. Remember, we are using an "S" word for each benefit to aid your memory. The Bible says forget not all of His benefits. Let us not forget any of His five-faceted benefits. The five "S" words to help us remember the benefits of redemption.

The first "S" is for Sin

The Name The Benefit

Jehovah-M'Kaddesh, Our Sanctification.

Jehovah-M'Kaddesh (pronounced Em Kaw-dash) means " the Lord who sanctifies (Leviticus 20:8). This is the most descriptive name of the character of God. Sanctification simply means separation from. God has separated you from the old evil nature and now you are a new person in Christ.

Many Christians think that they cannot live effectively in a world where there is so much evil. Well, God has provided separation from the evils of the present, negative world through His Name.

Simply say, "Praise Your Name for redeeming me from sin. Sin has no power over me, I am sanctified because you are Jehovah-M'Kaddesh. Jesus is my Jehovah-M'Kaddesh, my Sanctification." Confess His Name, thank and praise God that you are free from sin and sin consciousness. See it, say it, and pray it! **Sin is really no longer your problem!** It is His! Why? He is your Sanctification!

Lap #1 Our Father in heaven, Hallowed be Your Name

HOW TO HAVE PEACE AND LIVE WORRY FREE!

Where sin abounds, grace abounds much more. He gives more Grace. Today, we will continue to focus on confessing the five benefits revealed in His Name. As you recall, five is the number of grace, and the Names of God reveal to us the five-faceted grace of God to mankind in redemption. He loves you and wants you to experience His grace in five basic areas; these things belong to you by faith. It is up to you to declare and claim the benefits. We are using an "S" word for each benefit to help you remember. The Bible says forget not all of His benefits.

The Second "S" is Spirit.

The Name	**The Benefit**
Jehovah-Shalom	Our Peace
Jehovah-Shammah	Our Ever-Present One

22 And Gideon saw that he was the angel of Jehovah; and Gideon said, Alas, O Lord
Jehovah! forasmuch as I have seen the angel of Jehovah face to face. 23 And Jehovah
said unto him, Peace be unto thee; fear not: thou shalt not die. 24 Then Gideon built an
altar there unto Jehovah, and called it Jehovah-shalom: unto this day it is yet in Ophrah
of the Abiezrites. Judges 6:22-24 (American Standard Version)

Ezekiel 48:34-35 (paraphrased) says that the four sides of the city measure to a total of nearly six miles. "From now on the name of the city will be Yahweh or Jehovah-Shammah: 'God-Is-There.'"

First, remember you should declare the Name. Say, "You are Jehovah-Shalom! The Lord, my peace. I Praise and hallow Your Name for redeeming me from sin and giving me the fullness of Your Spirit. You have reconciled me by the blood of Jesus so I could receive the fullness of your Holy Spirit." Then boldly say, "You are the Spirit of Peace! Praise You Jehovah-Shalom, You are my Peace!"

Next, work on the Name Jehovah-Shammah with a similar pattern of confession and praise. Proclaim the Name Jehovah-Shammah and thank God for His presence. Acknowledge His benefit and thank God for the facet of redemption. Let today be a day of peace in His presence. Simply pray now ask God to awaken His Presence in your life. God is here to solve all of your problems and carry all of your worries and concerns today! The Lord Is There."

Confess your redemption today: "Lord, You are my Peace and I cast all of my cares, worries, and concerns on You today. I thank You that You are here to see me through to victory in every situation I face."

Lap #1 Our Father in heaven, Hallowed be Your Name

PRAYER BRINGS SECURITY & VICTORY!

Thank God for another wonderful day! Well, get a good cup of java if you like and let's go! Let's continue to focus on praising God for the five benefits revealed in His redemptive Names in prayer. Faith receives and declares the promises of God before they are manifested. Use your faith! Following our pattern of using an "S" word for each benefit, here is the third benefit of our redemption which is **Security**.

The third "S" is for Security.

The corresponding Names of God are:

The Name	The Benefit
Jehovah-Rohi	Our Shepherd
Jehovah-Nissi	Our Victory/Banner

The LORD is my shepherd; I shall not want. Psalm 23:1 (King James Version)

GOD TAKES CARE OF EVERYTHING! As the shepherd was out with his flocks he was completely responsible for their EVERYTHING—good pasture, still water (sheep are afraid of running noisy streams), care, discipline, and protection from every type of danger and wild animal attack. When David speaks of the Lord as his shepherd he is saying that he fully understands and calls upon the Lord to be his EVERYTHING. If the shepherd is a good one, the sheep are totally safe. Free from worry, they can graze from one tasty nibble to the next. They can rest and sleep without thought of being picked off. If they wander a bit too far from the flock, they can count on the shepherd's staff to reign them back in.

He is keeping watch continuously and he knows each of them by name. God is your security! Jesus said of himself, "I am the good shepherd. The good shepherd gives his life for the sheep," (John 10:11) and "I am the good shepherd; and I know my sheep, and am known by my own." (John 10:14)

GOD GUARANTEES YOU VICTORY!

Exodus 17:15 (American Standard Version) says, “15 And Moses built an altar, and called the name of it Jehovah-nissi; 16 And he said, Jehovah hath sworn: Jehovah will have war with Amalek from generation to generation.”

God is your victory! His love never fails. Since love never fails, love never loses. He is your Lover, Shepherd, and Victory. You never need to be insecure another day. He will take care of you and give you absolute victory today. While Joshua and the army of Israel fought the Amalekites in the valley below, Moses stood on the top of Mt. Horeb, which is Mt. Sinai, with his hands stretched out before the Lord, with his rod in his hands. The symbolism in this picture is full of instruction.

Moses lifted up his hands in prayer to God and held up the rod, which represented God's omnipotent power, so that all Israel could see it standing erect, like an immovable banner upon Mt. Sinai. But when Moses hands got heavy, the rod he held sagged. When the army of Israel could not see the rod, they wavered and the Amalekites prevailed against them. Aaron and Hur found a stone and put it under Moses to support him.

Then they stood by Moses and held up his hands until the going down of the sun. Thus, Israel defeated the Amalekites. We are like those Israelites. At times it seems that our spiritual warfare will surely end in defeat. Like Moses, we get weary. Our legs are feeble. Our hands begin to sag. It appears that we will surely fall to the enemy. But, just when we have no strength, Christ our High Priest, represented by Aaron, and the Spirit of God, represent by Hur, whose name means liberty, inspire us to lift up our hands in prayer to God.

PRAY & SAY!

Pray and say, "Lord, You are Jehovah-Rohi, the Lord my Shepherd. I praise and hallow Your Name for redeeming me from all insecurity and giving me your Divine protection. You have reconciled me by the blood of Jesus and given me abundance of security. I am so secure in You! You are my Shepherd and I do not want." Then say, "Praise You are Jehovah-Nissi! You are my banner, Your banner over me is love, and love never fails. That means You are my victory today." Now confess, "I am an overcomer by the blood of the Lamb and the word of my testimony or my confession of faith." Continue with a similar pattern of confession and praise. PROCLAIM! DECLARE! THANK! Proclaim the Name, declare the benefit, and thank God for the facet of redemption. Let today be a day of Divine security and freedom from fear of man, terrorism, or loss.
Confess your redemption today.

I am so secure! Lord, You are the good Shepherd. You gave Your life to bring security to Your sheep. I shall not fear or want because You are my victory!

Lap #1 Our Father in heaven, Hallowed be Your Name

PRAYER BRINGS SOUNDNESS & HEALTH

Dear friend, I pray that you may enjoy good health and that all may go well with you, even as your soul is getting along well. 3 John 1:2 (New International Version)

Confessing His Name in prayer should be becoming a habit for you now. You don't have to get spooky in prayer, just enjoy your fellowship with God; confess his Name and be thankful. Thankful people are always full of praise. You will grow stronger in faith as you give praise and glory to God. Today, let's continue in our focus on confessing or praising God for the five benefits. Remember, He loves you and wants you to experience His grace in five basic areas.

The fourth "S" is for Sickness

The Name	The Benefit
Jehovah-Rophe	Our Healer

"... For I am the LORD who heals you." Exodus 15:26 (New King James Version)

The Lord is a Healer! He said I am the LORD Who heals you to His people. First, you should declare the Name. Then say, "You are Jehovah-Rophe, The Lord my healer! I Praise Your Name for health, healing, and soundness, for redeeming me from sickness and disease and giving me Divine health. You have reconciled me by the blood of Jesus, so that I could live a life of Divine health. Praise Your Name! I have no fear of sickness and disease because by Jesus stripes or wounds, I am healed!" Continue with a similar pattern of confession and praise. So, proclaim the Name, declare the benefit, and thank God for healing, even while you are still sick. That's faith.

Continue to imagine the blood of Jesus as you praise Jehovah Rophe. The Blood of Jesus has healed you because He was beaten cruelly with the Roman whip and blood flowed from the stripes or wounds on His body. Praise Him for it in prayer! Let today be a day of soundness, of Divine health, of freedom from disease.

Confess your soundness today:
I confess that by His wounds I am healed. I feel happy, healthy and terrific because you are Jehovah-Rophe my soundness.

Lap #1 Our Father in heaven, Hallowed be Your Name

PRAYER BRINGS SUCCESS!

For ye know the grace of our Lord Jesus Christ, that, though He was rich, yet for your sakes He became poor, that ye through His poverty might be rich. 2 Corinthians 8:9 (King James Version)

Now, let's conclude our focus on confessing and praising the Name of God in prayer as it relates to the five benefits of redemption. We have come to the end of lap one of the prayer track. As you recall from previous lessons, five is the number of grace, and the Names of God reveal the five-faceted grace of God to man. The Father wants you to experience His grace in these five basic areas. Your prayer brings the manifestation of God's grace to pass.

The fifth "S" is for Success.

The Name	The Benefit
Jehovah-Jireh	Our Provider

14 And Abraham called the name of that place Jehovah-Jireh: as it is said to this day, In the mount of the LORD it shall be seen. Genesis 22:14 (King James Version)

I love this Name because it reveals God's desire for us to prosper. It literally means Jehovah "sees" and provides. A modern translation of Genesis 22:14 says, "And Abraham called the name of that place 'The Lord provides.' It is said to this day, 'In the mountain of the Lord provision will be made.'" God's Name is Jehovah-Jireh! The meaning of this name is The Lord Who Provides. The name is literally, The Lord Who Will See To It.

This is what we long for when we have a need that is personal and special: one who will see to our needs and provide for us. This is what Jehovah-Jireh means; the Lord Who will see to it that my every need is met. One Who knows my need because He sees. One Who is able to meet my need in just the right time as He did for Abraham, and One Who can meet it fully. For Abraham, it was the ram caught in the thicket that was offered in Isaac's place. For us it is whatever we need. So in prayer you confess, "You are Jehovah-Jireh, The Lord my provider! I praise Your Name for redeeming me from poverty and giving me Divine prosperity and abundance."

Confess, "You have reconciled me from lack and shortage by the blood of Jesus, so that I could live a life of Divine prosperity. Praise Your Name Jehovah-Jireh! You are the One who sees and provides for me. I have no fear of lack because Jesus wore a crown of thorns to redeem me from Adam's curse so that I could have material blessing." Continue with a similar pattern of confession and praise. Proclaim the Name, declare the benefit, and thank God for the facet of redemption.

Imagine the blood of Jesus that has redeemed you from poverty and lack as you praise Jehovah-Jireh. It is the Blood of Jesus that made you prosperous. Your confession of faith works an eternal value in you and produces prosperity. Praise Him for it. Today is a day of Divine prosperity and freedom from poverty and lack. Forget not all of His benefits.

Make this confession today: I confess today that my success in life is given to me by the grace of God. You are even making my mistakes succeed because of Your grace. I rest in financial prosperity and success. I have more than enough! Make it personal. Close your eyes and see your bills paid and needs met while you pray!

In whom we have redemption through His blood, the forgiveness of sins, according to the riches of His grace. Ephesians 1:7 (King James Version)

Lap #1 Our Father in heaven, Hallowed be Your name.

Running The Prayer Track

Lap #2 Your kingdom come. Your will be done, On earth as it is in heaven.

The Kingdom of God is God's way of doing things. The kingdom of God is the realm, rule and reign of the God of grace. You could say it is where the King, Jesus has dominion. Kingdom is synonymous with the King's dominion. The kingdom of God always comes when we yield ourselves to God. This lap of the prayer is where we acknowledge our brokenness before God. We are saying, you know what is best for me, my family, my Church, our nation, and this world. Thy kingdom come!

Acts 20:32 says, :And now, brethren, I commend you to God and to the word of His grace, which is able to build you up and give you an inheritance among all those who are sanctified." Notice that the Word is called The Word of His grace.

Matthew 13:19 says, "When anyone hears the word of the kingdom, and does not understand it, then the wicked one comes and snatches away what was sown in his heart. This is he who received seed by the wayside." Jesus calls it the Word of the kingdom.

Some have said that this prayer is not for the Church because the kingdom has already come to the church. They refer to what Paul said in Colossians chapter one as proof that we should not pray this. Colossians 1:12-14 says, "giving thanks to the Father who has qualified us to be partakers of the inheritance of the saints in the light. 13 He has delivered us from the power of darkness and conveyed us into the kingdom of the Son of His love, 14 in whom we have redemption through His blood, the forgiveness of sins." Even though it is true that legally the kingdom of God has come in the spirit realm as a result of the finished work of Jesus, we are still praying for the vital manifestation of that kingdom in the everyday, sense knowledge realm of life.

THE LEGAL AND THE VITAL

Many things are ours legally, in the spirit realm, but we must pray for them to become ours vitally in the natural world. This prayer is designed to demand that the legal become the vital. For example, a law may be legally on the books but not vitally executed even by lawmakers, such as the case of slavery in America. The slaves were legally emancipated by the Emancipation Proclamation, but not vitally free until demands were executed through the civil rights movement.

PRAY, YOUR KINGDOM COME!

Jesus instructed us to pray Your kingdom come, your will be done! We are to pray for the rule of grace and the perfect will of God in our lives. Romans 12:2 says, "And do not be conformed to this world, but be transformed by the renewing of your mind, that you may prove what is that good and acceptable and perfect will of God." Colossians 1:9 says, "For this reason we also, since the day we heard it, do not cease to pray for you, and to ask that you may be filled with the knowledge of His will in all wisdom and spiritual understanding." Paul prayed that the believers would be filled with the knowledge of the will of God. Also, we must pray for the kingdom and will of God because Satan is the god of this world. As believers we are living on hostile territory with an enemy arrayed against us. We actually live lives of daily combat with the god of this age.

THE GOD OF THIS AGE

2 Corinthians 4:4 says, "whose minds the god of this age has blinded, who do not believe, lest the light of the gospel of the glory of Christ, who is the image of God, should shine on them." Notice that the first mention of the word god starts with a small g. This is not talking about God the heavenly Father. It is talking about the evil ruler of this world. How did Satan become the god or ruler of this world? Well, to make it simple, God had given Adam a lease on the planet to rule and reign in this realm of the universe (like a kingdom) for a time.

When Adam committed high treason and betrayed God, he became the Benedict Arnold of the universe. When he did, he gave dominion over the planet to Satan. Satan now has Adam's lease. He will be the god of this world of age until Adam's lease is up and Jesus returns to set up His physical kingdom on the earth, a 1,000 year reign called the millennium. That is why we must pray and declare the kingdom of God come. When we do so, we are exercising our authority in the kingdom and the earth. We are not praying that Jesus would make the kingdom available to us as some have said, rather we are declaring and confessing God's dominion on this Satan infested planet!

Here are five areas that you should pray for the vital manifestation of God's will over each day:

1. Your personal life, dedication, and consecration to the will of God
2. Your family, spouse, future spouse, children, and parents
3. Your church, pastor, and congregation
4. Your nation, president, and other political leaders
5. The world, evangelize of the nations

Today, pray, proclaim and decree, Your kingdom come, your will be done!

Lap #2 Your kingdom come. Your will be done, On earth as it is in heaven.

Running The Prayer Track

Lap #3 Give us this day our daily bread.

Blessed is the man that walketh not in the counsel of the ungodly, nor standeth in the way of sinners, nor sitteth in the seat of the scornful. But his delight is in the law of the LORD; and in his law doth he meditate day and night. And he shall be like a tree planted by the rivers of water, that bringeth forth his fruit in his season; his leaf also shall not wither; and whatsoever he doeth shall prosper. Psalm 1:1-3 (King James Version)

I want to take some time on this lap of prayer because money or material provision is such an important part of our lives. Satan will fight you more in the realm of finances than in any other realm. Why? It's simple. He wants to keep money out of the hands of Christians and churches. God wants to prosper individual Christians and churches. This is why we must pray.

God's will is prosperity, so He naturally desires to give you your daily bread or provision. Now, you are probably thinking;, well, if His will is prosperity, why do I have to pray for my needs to be met? The reason you have to pray is that God demands faith of you and He told you to *ask*. James 4:2 said, "you have not, because you ask not." James also said that you must ask in faith. James 1:6 says, "But let him ask in faith, nothing wavering..."

Faith comes by hearing by the Word of God. So I want to give you some verses about prosperity on which to meditate and build a capacity for faith.

The Bible teaches that meditation is an important key to prosperity in Psalm 1:1-3 and Joshua 1:8. Please look up each of the verses and highlight them in your own Bible. This will be one of the most important actions you will ever take to improve your financial situation. God is ready to bless you and manifest His prosperity in your present trouble. Believe it, conceive it, and receive it! God? Will is prosperity! Confess this now, God's Will is my prosperity, I receive my daily bread!

Prosperity Scriptures

1. **Joshua 1:8—**I have prosperity and good success
2. **Psalm 1:1-3—**Whatever I do prospers
3. **John 10:10—**I have abundant life…
4. **2 Corinthians** 9:6-8—I sow (give) bountifully and reap bountifully
5. **Galatians 3:13-14—**I am redeemed from the curse of the law
6. **3 John 2—**I prosper financially and live in health

Philippians 4:19 says, "But my God shall supply all your needs according to His riches in glory by Christ Jesus." **God sees every human need.** Not only does He see our needs, He also wants us to live prosperous lives; God's will is prosperity. He actually wants us to prosper financially and live the abundant life.

God said He would supply all of your needs according to His riches in glory by Christ Jesus. Why are so many Christians bankrupt? Why are so many struggling to make ends meet? Primarily, it is due to a negative confession concerning finances. You hear people say, "I just cant seem to get ahead, I will never get out of all of this debt." Some people would rather try to figure out why they are struggling on their own rather than to pray and confess the Word. Your mental solution is usually only a temporary solution. God's provision through prayer is a Divine, eternal solution. God's will is prosperity; however, you must believe and confess His Word for your daily needs to be met in your life. As you enjoy His presence today, consider God as Jehovah-Jireh, the One Who sees and provides!

PRAY FOR THE WEALTH OF OTHERS

Proverbs 19:17 says, **"**He that hath pity upon the poor lendeth unto the LORD; and that which he hath given will He pay him again."

The Bible teaches that we are to seek the wealth of others, not just our own wealth. I think this is one of the greatest challenges for people that start to enjoy prosperity. Why? They often become covetous. The Bible teaches that we are to remember the poor always and that we are also to pray for the needs of others.

People often have material needs that are met because someone else prayed for them. Maybe their faith is weak, or maybe they have no faith at all. The Bible says that not all people have faith. 2 Thessalonians 3:1-2 says, "Finally, brethren, pray for us, that the word of the Lord may run *swiftly* and be glorified, just as *it is* with you, 2 and that we may be delivered from unreasonable and wicked men; **for not all have faith."**

Start with your immediate family members, then move to extended family, then friends and associates. You should also spend some time confessing provision for the needs of poor people in our nation and other countries—especially third world nations.
Don't be a selfish person when it comes to provision. Pray for the material needs of others in poor, third world countries. It will come back to you when you have pity on the poor. God uses some in the special gift of giving. Pray about this. God knows we need more givers in light of the present state of the Church where so many are seeking their own personal wealth only. **Seek the wealth of others, not just your own.** Pray and confess that God will heal our land and our economy!

CLAIMING WHAT YOU NEED IN PRAYER

God is Jehovah-Jireh but you must claim what you need! Genesis 22:14 from the New King James Version says, “And Abraham called the name of the place, The-LORD-Will-Provide; as it is said *to* this day, In the Mount of the LORD it shall be provided.” I like that translation; The-LORD-Will-Provide! You must declare that and rest in faith! Even though God sees your need, you must still confess or claim that you have what you need! He *sees* every human need. Some ask, why then, does He not provide for all of the needy people on the planet? It is simple: He has told us to pray for material provision. The key to having what you need is a focused, intelligent, Biblical kind of prayer and confession. *What do you need?* Are there areas of material need that you have not addressed to God?

Our Great Father God, would love to meet your needs abundantly above what you ask or think. Your daily confession should be; my God supplies all of my needs according to His riches in glory (Philippians 4:19). You must confess it and claim it. **Claim the material things you need.** God sees and He will provide! **Remember,** not only does He see our needs, he also wants us to live prosperous lives. God’s will is prosperity. He wants us to prosper financially and not just get by. Even though God’s will is prosperity, you must pray for the manifestation of what you need daily! As you go your way today, consider God as Jehovah-Jireh!

CONFESSING PROVISION

Ephesians 3:20 from the Amplified Bible says, "Now to Him Who, by (in consequence of) the [action of His] power that is at work within us, is able to [carry out His purpose and] do super-abundantly, far over and above all that we [dare] ask or think [infinitely beyond our highest prayers, desires, thoughts, hopes or dreams]." **Money comes to those who pray and act on the Word of God**! Those who carry out His purpose and pray prosper financially! I am talking about super-abundant, supernatural provision, not just doing a job and getting paid for it (which is okay, since God has said that we should work). Divine provision supersedes the economy and the world's system of finance. God is not limited by the economy or subject to it. What I am talking about is Divine prosperity, not man's limited financial wisdom. Man's financial wisdom is always limited.

God is able to do exceeding, abundantly beyond what we ask or think. That is supernatural! He wants you to experience supernatural provision. Remember the manna in the wilderness? It was provided supernaturally every day.

GOD WANTS YOU TO HAVE MONEY

Understand that God is not against you having money, but He is just against money having you! The reason I want to address money is that the Bible says it answers all things. Money is important in this life. Obviously, there are many things more important than money. However, in today's world, money is a necessity! Motivational speaker Les Brown has said, "Money is not everything, but it is right up there with oxygen." Prayer, confession and faith will produce the money you need. Money comes to those who say it, pray for it, and obey God's instructions about it.

MONEY IS GOD'S BLESSING!

Money is good! In the world we live in, money is a necessity! Even Jesus had a treasurer! Prayer and faith can produce financial blessing. God's Will is material blessing, because Christ redeemed us from the curse of the law so that the blessing of Abraham might come to us through Christ Jesus. The word curse means to empower to fail, while the word bless means to empower to prosperity. Here is an outline from the Bible of the blessing of Abraham from Deuteronomy chapter 28:12-13. It says, "The LORD will open the heavens, the storehouse of his bounty, to send rain on your land in season and to bless all the work of your hands. You will lend to many nations but will borrow from none. 13 The LORD will make you the head, not the tail."

BLESSING!

In its basic form, blessing means to say something good about something, just as cursing is to say something bad about something or someone. Remember, blessing is in the power of the tongue! The Bible says that Jesus blessed the loaves and they multiplied. He said something good over what appeared to be not enough and it became *more than enough!* Make your continual prayer and confession one of blessing.

Blessing belongs to you! Say something good over your finances NOW! Finally, in order to have the prosperity that God has for you it is important that you are in His will. God blesses those who are willing and obedient to Him. God will bless you with the best as you pray and obey.

If you are willing and obedient, you will eat the best from the land.
Isaiah 1:19 (New International Version)

Lap #3 Give us this day our daily bread.

Running The Prayer Track

Lap #4 And forgive us our debts, As we forgive our debtors.

The Lord teaches us the importance and power of forgiveness in prayer. In fact, Jesus regularly taught on this topic. Unforgiveness is the only sin that Jesus directly attached to unanswered prayer, according to my research. Many Christians will get all over someone about sins of the flesh while they are themselves living in unforgiveness. Remember, unforgiveness is a sin of the heart. God will judge you quicker for sins of the heart than sins of the flesh. If you walk in bitterness and unforgiveness toward people that have offended you, you are in a spiritual *danger zone*. All sin is bad, but sins of the heart outweigh sins of the flesh. God did not say if you smoke a cigarette you will not be forgiven. But He did say if you DO NOT FORGIVE, you will not be forgiven!

Mark 11:24-25 says, "Therefore I say to you, whatever things you ask when you pray, believe that you receive them, and you will have them. 25 'And whenever you stand praying, if you have anything against anyone, forgive him, that your Father in heaven may also forgive you your trespasses. 26 But if you do not forgive, neither will your Father in heaven forgive your trespasses.'"

Unforgiveness is a sin because it goes directly against the nature of God. His nature is Love! He is forgiving! That's why we must pray. Forgive us our debts, as we forgive our debtors! This is a critical lap on our prayer track.

JESUS TAUGHT FORGIVENESS

Jesus taught a lot about forgiveness and unforgiveness. Why? Because unforgiveness hinders our prayers and He wants us to receive answers to prayer. You can't live in unforgiveness without your heart condemning you. If your heart condemns you it will weaken your faith. When your faith is weak you often fail to receive what you prayed for. So you ask, "what do I do then Bernard?" Here is my advice: Forgive those who have offended you and get back into the light, and He is in the light. You can do this by fervent prayer. *Forgive us our debts, as we forgive our debtors.*

Get unforgiveness out of your life and STAND YOUR GROUND against the enemy. Do what Jesus said to do. Jesus said to pray forgive us our debts, as we forgive our debtors. Forgive, and you will be forgiven. Luke 6:37-38 (NIV) says, "Give and it will be given to you. A good measure, pressed down, shaken together and running over, will be poured into your lap. For with the measure you use, it will be measured to you."

GIVERS ARE FORGIVING

Notice how Jesus ties *giving* to *forgiving*? The last word in verse 37 is forgiven the first word in verse 38 is give. Listen to your heart right now and obey the directions that come from within concerning giving. So many of life's problems start with us becoming UNFORGIVING, or not in favor of giving. That is when you become critical, judgmental, bitter, stingy, and selfish. Don't get bitter, *GET BETTER!* Be like Jesus; forgive and give today and when you lay your head on the pillow tonight your sleep will be sweet because your heart will not be condemning you. Let's clean up the pipeline and get the blessings flowing into your life once again! We have seen that Jesus taught unforgiveness as the kingpin in unanswered prayer. Why? Faith will not work in an unforgiving heart. Learn to pray for forgiveness and forgive others today and watch your faith soar.

Lap #4 And forgive us our debts, As we forgive our debtors.

Running The Prayer Track

Lap #5 And do not lead us into temptation, But deliver us from the evil one.

"You intended to harm me, but God intended it for good to accomplish what is now being done, the saving of many lives." Genesis 50:20 (New International Version)

The King James Bible of Genesis 50:20 says, "But as for you, ye thought evil against me; but God meant it unto good..." The lesson is that God often brings good out of evil. The original Greek in this part of the Lord's Prayer says deliver us from the evil one, not deliver us from evil.

Some definitions of the word **devil** are: Satan; chief spirit of evil and adversary of God; tempter of mankind; master of Hell; an evil supernatural being. Satan or the devil is obviously the evil one.

God will not let the evil one (Satan) destroy or harm us with evil if we will pray. **Even if the world tries to harm us, God changes it for our good.**

GOOD IS NOT AUTOMATIC

Nevertheless, this wonderful God we serve never permits good for us automatically. THIS IS WHY WE MUST PRAY! We will often go through tests and trials before we experience God's goodness, like Joseph did. The land flowing with milk and honey is on the other side of the wilderness, not on this side. You must often pass through the desert of tests, trials, and temptations before you experience God's goodness.

Deuteronomy 8:2-3 says, "Remember how the LORD your God led you all the way in the desert these forty years, to humble you and to test you in order to know what was in your heart, whether or not you would keep his commands. He humbled you, causing you to hunger and then feeding you with manna, which neither you nor your fathers had known, to teach you that man does not live on bread alone but on every word that comes from the mouth of the LORD." The key to overcoming temptation and evil is in prayer.

GOD'S DISCIPLINE

Deuteronomy 8:15-16 says, "He led you through the vast and dreadful desert, that thirsty and waterless land, with its venomous snakes and scorpions. He brought you water out of hard rock. He gave you manna to eat in the desert, something your fathers had never known, to *humble* and to test you so that in the end it might go well with you." The reason why God has disciplined you and led you through the desert is to bless you in the end.

Without passing through the desert of temptation and trials, you will not be ready for blessings.

In the Bible, David killed Goliath to become a hero in all of Israel and was later enthroned as king, but he was only a young shepherd boy when he confronted Goliath. He was even neglected in his family. The gigantic enemy, Goliath, stood between the shepherd David and the king David. He could become king after defeating Goliath. What is the Goliath you are facing today? You can conquer him with prayer. **Therefore, we must expect that temptation, trials, and tribulation will turn into great blessings as we pray. Lead us not into temptation, but deliver us from the evil one.**

JESUS KNOWS HOW WE FEEL

Jesus loved us, obeyed God, and He came to earth as a man. He lived on earth for 33 years, took away our sins, and endured *extreme* pain on the Cross. God led Jesus to the way of suffering or temptation through which forgiveness, salvation, and heaven could reach us.

God continually delivered Jesus from the evil one while He was living upon the earth. Jesus was crucified on the Cross, and His blood was shed to forgive our sins and save us. Therefore, **Jesus fully knows how we feel in the midst of temptation and suffering.**

He can deliver us from the pain of sin, disease, and circumstances, for He has already passed through them. Since He has already completely paid the price, He can help us. Hebrews 2:18 says, "For in that He Himself has suffered, being tempted, He is able to aid those who are tempted. Even though He understands what we are going through He still commands us to pray when suffering or trouble strikes.

Is anyone among you suffering? Let him pray. Is anyone cheerful? Let him sing psalms. (James 5:13 New King James Version)

GOD EXALTS THE HUMBLE

Human beings in general are arrogant. Nevertheless, when suffering comes, they realize how awful and terrible they are and become humble. It is only when we become humble that we can truly pray. The Lord hears the prayers of the humble. 1 Peter 5:6 says, "Humble yourselves, therefore, under God's mighty hand, that he may lift you up in due time."

God will lift us up if we humble ourselves by being broken. The more trials and temptations we experience with the attitude of prayer, the more humble we will be.

Those who are extremely obstinate and want to have their own way all the time will repent, be broken, obedient, cry out to God, and pray as they pass through trials and temptation. Hebrews 5:8-9 says, "Although he was a son, he learned obedience from what he suffered and, once made perfect, he became the source of eternal salvation for all who obey him." The Bible pattern is suffering and then perfection. 1 Peter 5:10 says, "And the God of all grace, who called you to his eternal glory in Christ, after you have suffered a little while, will himself restore you and make you strong, firm and steadfast." Suffering makes us strong, firm, and steadfast as we go through suffering prayerfully.

PRAYER DELIVERS FROM TROUBLE

James 5:13 says, "Is any one of you in trouble? He should pray. Is anyone happy? Let him sing songs of praise." Psalm 50:15 says, "and call upon me in the day of trouble; I will deliver you, and you will honor me."

When we call upon God in tribulation, God will deliver us. John Bunyan said, "Trials and tribulation make us seek God."

Psalm 23:5 says, "You prepare a table before me in the presence of my enemies. You anoint my head with oil; my cup overflows." God will spread a table only in the presence of your enemies. If your enemies are absent, there will be no table, no anointing and blessing, and no overflowing cup. Therefore, an easygoing life seems to be good temporarily, but it will not benefit you permanently. God's harsh training, that makes you pass through trials, and tribulation, will build you into strong, bold, and firm

Christians who may enjoy good health, that all may go well with you, even as your soul is getting along well.

PUT ON YOUR ARMOR

We are commanded to put on the whole armor of God in our daily combat with the forces of evil. The whole armor of God is like God's clothing. We are to put on or be clothed with the Lord Jesus Christ daily in prayer. Ephesians shows us how to be dressed to killed, as Rick Renner says.

Ephesians 6:10-18 reveals the armor of God:

1. Loins girded about with TRUTH
2. Breastplate of RIGHTEOUSNESS
3. Feet shod with the PREPARATION (READINESS) OF THE GOSPEL OF PEACE
4. Shield of FAITH
5. Helmet of SALVATION
6. Sword of the Spirit, which is the WORD OF GOD

As you are fully armed, pray protection for yourself and your family. He is your refuge, your fortress, your God! *Declare it now!*

"If I fail to spend two hours in prayer each morning, the devil gets the victory through the day. I have so much business I cannot get on without spending three hours daily in prayer." -- Martin Luther

CONFESS YOUR DELIVERANCE!

I encourage you to read Psalm 91 out loud and confess it over your life today. Psalm 91:14-16 (KJV) says, "14 Because he hath set his love upon me, therefore will I deliver him: I will set him on high, because he hath known my name. 15 He shall call upon me, and I will answer him: I will be with him in trouble; I will deliver him, and honour him. 16 With long life will I satisfy him, and show him my salvation."

Lap #5 And do not lead us into temptation, But deliver us from the evil one.

Running The Prayer Track

Lap #6 For Yours is the kingdom and the power and the glory forever.

Thine, O LORD, is the greatness, and the power, and the glory, and the victory, and the majesty: for all that is in the heaven and in the earth is thine; thine is the kingdom, O LORD, and thou art exalted as head above all. 1 Chronicles 29:11 (King James Version)

We have come to the sixth and final lap of the prayer track. The final lap is where we declare to God that *Yours* is the kingdom, the power, and the glory. These final words of the prayer have a threefold function. First, these words are a confession of our faith in God's will. It is only when we do God's will that we will see the realization of His kingdom and the glorification of His Name. When we conclude the prayer by confessing that the kingdom belongs to God, that we are certain of His power and glory, we conclude with words that express our faith in His work to accomplish His will, and establish the kingdom. We trust that His kingdom will come in His good time for the sake of His glory. We believe that He and He alone will make it come to pass.

A DECLARATION OF FAITH

The confession of our faith in the kingdom is important. It must be an intelligent confession of what we really believe that God is doing in this world. Praying the Lord's prayer is to confess that God rules His kingdom with power. The confession at the end of the prayer is a confession that someday God will conclude history in Jesus' favor.

WORDS OF PRAISE

The final words of the Lord's prayer are words of praise. Notice that the prayer track starts with praise and ends with praise. We start out by honoring God's Name and end by declaring His glory! *The kingdom, the power, and the glory is yours!*

To confess our faith in His kingdom, power, and glory, is also to praise Him for His kingdom, power, and glory. Praise and confession are actually inseparable. Ending the prayer with words of praise that express our confidence in Him is also a way of casting ourselves upon Him for the accomplishment of all. On the one hand, the Lord's prayer teaches us to seek more earnestly God's kingdom, but on the other hand, it also reminds us that the kingdom is His. Ending the prayer this way reminds us that He will bring it to pass by the power that only He possesses. It is His glory that is at stake. It is His will for us to praise Him, for His power and glory then is also for us to rest in Him for the fulfillment of the kingdom.

To praise Him and rest in Him means that we are enjoying Him. When we repeatedly pray, "Thine is the kingdom and the power and glory for ever and ever," we learn to relish the fact that He is in charge. His mysterious plan is perfect and guides all things toward His kingdom and glory. *His power rules over all. AMEN!*

CONCLUSION

As we conclude our prayer track journey, I urge you to make this confession of praise from the book of Psalms 108 :1-4 personal: “O God, my heart is fixed; I will sing and give praise, even with my glory. Awake, psaltery and harp: I myself will awake early. I will praise thee, O LORD, among the people: and I will sing praises unto thee among the nations. For thy mercy is great above the heavens: and thy truth reacheth unto the clouds.”

Lap #6 For Yours is the kingdom and the power and the glory forever. Amen.

FINAL NOTE: TERRORISM & THE 21ST CENTURY

One thing we all seem to agree on is that 9/11 changed the world. What would you give to know that you and your loved ones are completely free from the present threat of terrorism? Terrorism is a manifestation of evil in the modern age. Victory over terrorism belongs to the praying believer.

You must prayerfully confess God's Word for protection of yourself and your loved ones. There is not a lot of talk about confession for protection today, but I believe it is crucial. Why? We live in what the Bible calls perilous times. The Bible declares that no weapon formed against us will prosper. Well, terrorism is certainly a weapon formed against humanity. In the age of fear and threats of terrorism we live in, you should pray and confess the Word daily over your spouse, immediate family, extended family, friends, associates, and nation. Terrorism operates by and promotes the spirit of fear. God does not give us a spirit of fear! The Bible says that we will be far from oppression and terror shall not come near us. Pray and confess the Word daily for Divine protection and intervention of God into the affairs of our nation against the forces of terrorism.

Isaiah 54:14 says, *"In righteousness shalt thou be established thou shalt be far from oppression; for thou shalt not fear: and from terror; for it shall not come near thee. TERROR SHALL NOT COME NEAR . . ."*

About the Author

Bernard Smalls

Bernard Smalls is a Christian minister who is an anointed teacher of the Word of God. Mr. Smalls functioned as a corporate trainer in the business world and was a consulting resource with a focus on leadership, sales, and service excellence. Bernard teaches biblical yet practical principles, with the serving heart being the key to perpetual prosperity in any organization. He was a professional drummer playing in the Bay Area striving to make it big on the West Coast. After a potentially lucrative deal with Motown fell through, his bass player handed him some Christian books; shortly after which, he accepted Jesus as Lord. Later on, he moved to Alaska where he attended Charismatic Bible College of Alaska and entered the ministry full-time. He and his wife Karen founded Prevailing Word Outreach Church in Anchorage, a Church which had a tremendous impact on the state of Alaska. He is also the founder of Prevailing Word City Church in Atlanta, Georgia.

www.goteachfaith.com

Contact Info:
Abinadab's Project
Bernard Smalls
P.O. Box 724
Suwanee, Georgia 30024
email: gunghoguru@hotmail.com

Call to Me, and I will answer you, and show you great and mighty things, which you do not know. **Jeremiah 33: 3**

www.ingramcontent.com/pod-product-compliance
Ingram Content Group UK Ltd.
Pitfield, Milton Keynes, MK11 3LW, UK
UKHW051137260726
13967UKWH00010B/3096